D1087458

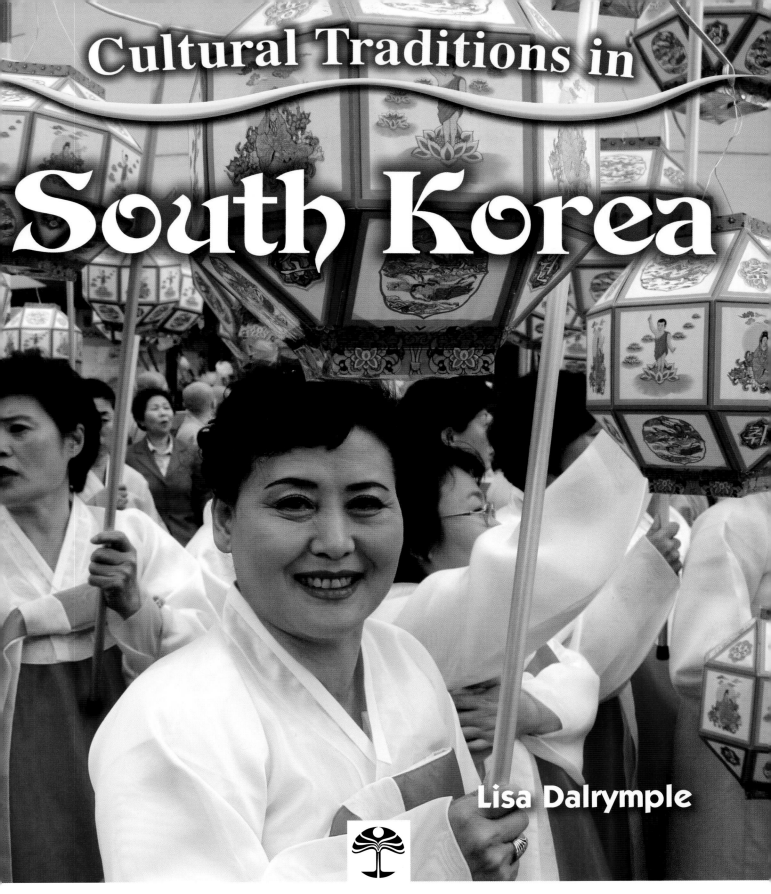

Cultural Traditions in
South Korea

Lisa Dalrymple

Crabtree Publishing Company
www.crabtreebooks.com

Crabtree Publishing Company
www.crabtreebooks.com

Author: Lisa Dalrymple

Publishing plan research and development:
Reagan Miller

Editorial director: Kathy Middleton

Editors: Janine Deschenes, Crystal Sikkens

Proofreader and indexer: Petrice Custance

Photo research: Crystal Sikkens, Tammy McGarr

Designer: Tammy McGarr

Production coordinator and prepress technician:
Tammy McGarr

Print coordinator: Katherine Berti

Cover: Cherry blossoms (top); Gyeongbokgung palace in Seoul, South Korea (background); Pink hibiscus, South Korea's national flower (bottom right); Tteok, traditional cakes made from rice (bottom right); Sand sculpture from Busan Sand Festival in Busan, South Korea (bottom center); Traditional dish, mixed rice bibimbap (bottom left); Buk, traditional drum (bottom left); Dancer performing Taepyeongmu, a dance for peace (center)

Title page: People celebrating the Lotus Lantern Parade for Buddha's birthday in Seoul, South Korea

Photographs:
Alamy: © Yooniq Images: p9; © epa european pressphoto agency b.v: pp 10 (top left), 11, 25; © MarioPonta: p22;
AP Images: Ahn Young-joon: pp 26, 27;
Creative Commons: Korea.net: pp 16–17 (bottom), 21 (top), 30 (bottom); cover (bottom right)
Getty: JUNG YEON-JE: p12; Chung Sung-Jun: p13;
iStock: © Kevin Landwer-Johan: p31 (middle left)
Thinkstock: Credit: theJIPEN: (middle left)
Shutterstock: © Bikeworldtravel: cover (center); © Gina Smith: title page, p31 (bottom left); © Narongsak Nagadhana: p5; © mastapiece: pp14–15 (bkgd); © Artaporn Puthikampol: p20; © wasanajai: p24; © yochika photographer: p28 (bottom right); © Guitar photographer: p29; © wizdata: p31 (top right)

All other images by Shutterstock

Library and Archives Canada Cataloguing in Publication

Dalrymple, Lisa, author
    Cultural traditions in South Korea / Lisa Dalrymple.

(Cultural traditions in my world)
Includes index.
Issued in print and electronic formats.
ISBN 978-0-7787-8088-5 (bound).--
ISBN 978-0-7787-8092-2 (paperback).--
ISBN 978-1-4271-8094-0 (html)

    1. Festivals--Korea (South)--Juvenile literature. 2. Holidays--Korea (South)--Juvenile literature. 3. Korea (South)--Social life and customs--Juvenile literature. 4. Korea (South)--Civilization--Juvenile literature. I. Title. II. Series: Cultural traditions in my world

GT4886.K6D35 2016   j394.2695195   C2015-907459-2
                                         C2015-907460-6

Library of Congress Cataloging-in-Publication Data

Names: Dalrymple, Lisa, author.
Title: Cultural Traditions in South Korea / Lisa Dalrymple.
Description: New York : Crabtree Pub., 2016. | Series: Cultural Traditions in My World | Includes index. | Description based on print version record and CIP data provided by publisher; resource not viewed.
Identifiers: LCCN 2015047435 (print) | LCCN 2015042103 (ebook) | ISBN 9781427180940 (electronic HTML) | ISBN 9780778780885 (reinforced library binding : alk. paper) | ISBN 9780778780922 (pbk. : alk. paper)
Subjects: LCSH: Holidays--Korea (South)--Juvenile literature. | Festivals--Korea (South)--Juvenile literature. | Korea (South)--Social life and customs--Juvenile literature.
Classification: LCC GT4886.K6 (print) | LCC GT4886.K6 D35 2016 (ebook) | DDC 394.2695195--dc23
LC record available at http://lccn.loc.gov/2015047435

Crabtree Publishing Company
www.crabtreebooks.com   1-800-387-7650

Printed in Canada/022016/IH20151223

Published in Canada
Crabtree Publishing
616 Welland Ave.
St. Catharines, ON
L2M 5V6

Published in the United States
Crabtree Publishing
PMB 59051
350 Fifth Avenue, 59th Floor
New York, New York 10118

Published in the United Kingdom
Crabtree Publishing
Maritime House
Basin Road North, Hove
BN41 1WR

Published in Australia
Crabtree Publishing
3 Charles Street
Coburg North
VIC 3058

Contents

Welcome to South Korea

South Korea has a history that goes back over 4,000 years! It shares a **peninsula** near China with North Korea. Some of South Korea's traditions come from its long relationship with China. Life in South Korea is influenced by the teachings of Confucius, an ancient Chinese thinker.

The Pacific Ocean surrounds three sides of South Korea.

South Korea is a thriving, modern country. Today, most people live in cities.

People in South Korea have great respect for the spirits of their ancestors. They ask them to help guide life today. South Korea's most important holidays began as **rural** festivals. At festival time, people return to their birthplace in the country to visit their parents and grandparents.

The Bridge of Freedom connects North and South Korea. At the border, South Koreans have hung colored ribbons with messages to show their love for their North Korean ancestors, both living and dead.

Happy New Year!

Fireworks for Korean New Year explode over the Seoul Tower in Seoul, South Korea's capital city.

South Korea follows the solar calendar, which runs from January to December, as well as the lunar calendar. The lunar calendar is based on the 12 cycles of the Moon. The New Year's Day holiday in South Korea is on January 1, just like in North America. However, celebrations for the Korean New Year don't take place until the first day of the first lunar month, which falls in either January or February.

During Korean New Year, people have three days off. Workers in the city often travel back to their family homes to celebrate. On New Year's Day, children show respect to their parents and grandparents by bowing to them. In return, the elders give them money in silk pouches. Later in the day, people celebrate with parties, or by playing traditional board games and flying kites.

Everyone wears new clothes for a fresh year. Some people wear traditional Korean clothes called *hanbok*.

Did You Know?
In South Korea, it is believed that people turn one year older on New Year's when they eat the traditional *Tteokguk* soup!

Birthdays

One of the first celebrations in a Korean baby's life is the One Hundred Day celebration. This takes place when the baby is 100 days old, which is just over three months. The family thanks the spirits of their grandmothers for protecting the child. They also pray for the child's health and safety in the future.

One year after a baby is born, the child celebrates their first birthday. On this day, the baby is seated at a table with many objects. The first thing the baby grabs is believed to show their future. They might become a **scholar** if they grab a pencil, or a business person if they grab money.

A person's 60th, 70th, and 80th birthdays are important **milestone** birthdays. They are often celebrated with a large party and a feast that includes fruit, rice cakes, and traditional cookies. Many people also celebrate these birthdays by going on a trip overseas or by donating money to people in need.

When a person turns 60 years old, it means they have lived one entire cycle of the lunar calendar.

9

Celebrating Love

In South Korea, Valentine's Day is also called Red Day. On this day, February 14, girls give chocolate to boys. Boys give candy and gifts back to the girls on White Day, which is March 14. April 14, or Black Day, is for anyone who did not get Red or White Day gifts. People on this day enjoy a special dinner featuring noodles.

In honor of Valentine's Day, a store in Seoul created a shoe almost 7 feet (2 m) high out of 132 pounds (60 kg) of chocolate.

Jajangmyeon is a traditional Black Day dish made with noodles in black bean sauce.

On May 8, families celebrate Parents' Day. Children often give their parents flowers called carnations, which are a symbol of love and respect. They might also buy presents or make cards and crafts for them at school. Families spend time together doing things that parents enjoy. They visit parks and museums, or go out for a special dinner.

Did You Know?
In South Korea, there is no Mother's Day or Father's Day. Both are celebrated on Parents' Day.

As part of an event celebrating Parents' Day, children pin carnations on seniors.

Independence and Liberation Days

Japan controlled Korea from 1910 to 1945. In 1919, many Koreans organized **protests** against the Japanese government. Over 7,500 people were killed by Japanese soldiers and thousands more were wounded as a result of the protests. This sparked the beginning of Korea's independence **movement**. To honor this fight for freedom, Koreans celebrate Independence Movement Day on March 1.

Students in Seoul proudly wave the South Korean flag while participating in a parade in celebration of Independence Movement Day.

South Korean dancers perform during a Liberation Day ceremony in Seoul.

Gwangbokjeol, or Liberation Day, celebrates the end of World War II, when Japan lost control of Korea. On August 15, people attend ceremonies and parades, and they sing a special *Gwangbokjeol* song, which is about protecting the beauty of South Korea forever. In honor of the protestors who died during the Independence Movement, their ancestors are allowed to visit museums and other public places for free.

Children's Day

May 5 is the day Korean children wait for all year long. It's Children's Day! Their parents give them presents and the whole day is about family fun! Schools and many places of work are closed.

On Children's Day, parents take their children to fun places such as zoos, parks, and movie theaters.

14

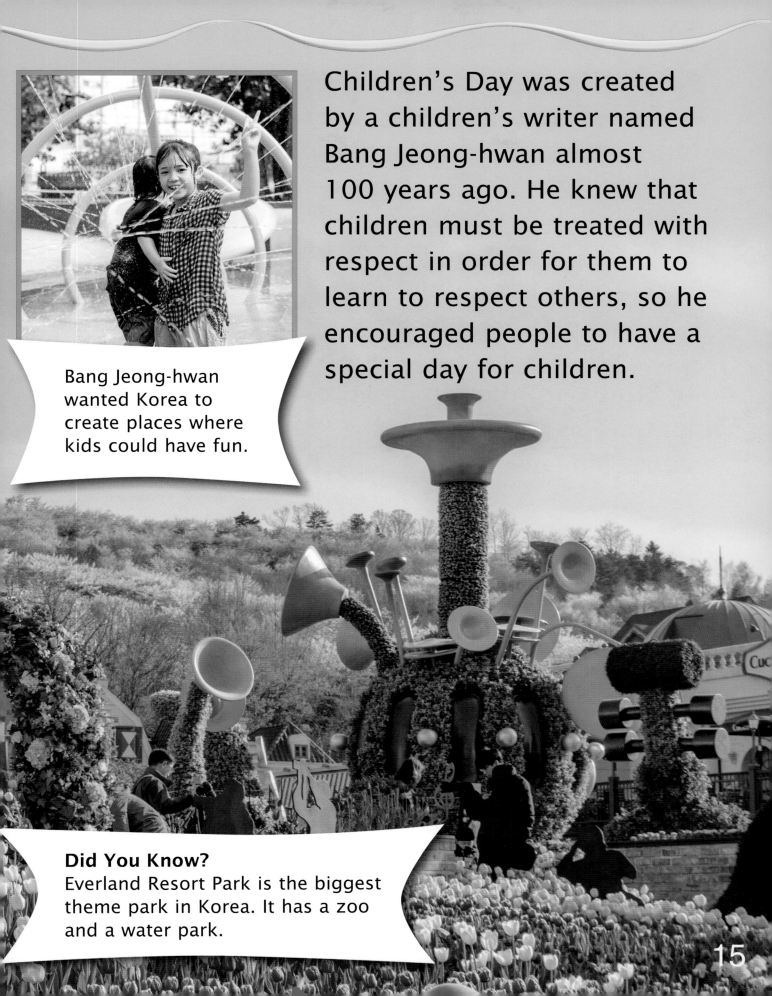

Children's Day was created by a children's writer named Bang Jeong-hwan almost 100 years ago. He knew that children must be treated with respect in order for them to learn to respect others, so he encouraged people to have a special day for children.

Bang Jeong-hwan wanted Korea to create places where kids could have fun.

Did You Know?
Everland Resort Park is the biggest theme park in Korea. It has a zoo and a water park.

15

Buddha's Birthday

Buddhism is the main religion in South Korea. It follows the teachings of Buddha, a monk who lived in India hundreds of years ago. Buddha's birthday is on the 8th day of the 4th lunar month. This is usually in the middle of May.

On Buddha's Birthday, some temples serve a rice dish with vegetables called *bibimbap*. Sometimes there is an egg or meat on top.

In celebration of Buddha's birthday, homes, streets, and temples are decorated with colorful paper lanterns. Buddhists visit temples to worship. When they are done, they are served tea and a free meal. Many people travel to Seoul for the Lotus Lantern Festival. The highlight of the festival is a parade that makes its way to the Joygesa Temple.

Did You Know?
For good luck, some people write out a prayer and slip it into a paper lantern decoration.

The Lotus Lantern Parade happens at night. There are many colorful floats and thousands of glowing lanterns.

Teachers' Day

Education and knowledge are very important in South Korea. Teachers are highly respected, and to honor them a special holiday known as Teachers' Day was created. This holiday is celebrated on May 15, which is the birthday of King Sejong the Great. He ruled Korea in the early 1400s. King Sejong developed a new Korean alphabet so that everyone could learn to read.

In Seoul, there is a bronze statue honoring King Sejong. It weighs 20 tons (18 metric tons) and is over 20 feet (6m) tall!

On Teachers' Day, schools throw parties for their teachers. Children make special cards and parents send gifts. Sometimes former students will return to their old schools and surprise their teachers with gifts and flowers. Schools might have classes for only half of the day so the teachers can go home early.

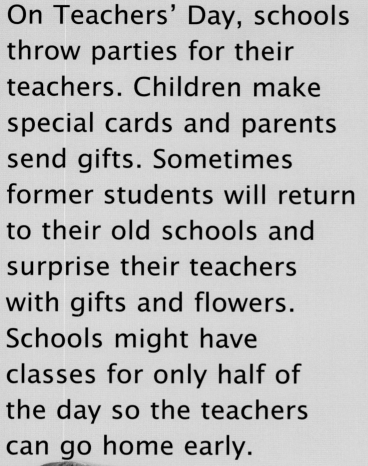

Carnations are a symbol of respect in South Korea. Students give them to their teachers on Teachers' Day

Memorial Day

Memorial Day is on June 6. People remember the Korean men and women who died in war or in the Independence Movement. There are still South Korean soldiers defending the border with North Korea. Many students write letters to thank them. Others make posters honoring past soldiers.

Flowers and a flag are placed on soldiers' graves. People also leave offerings of traditional food such as rice cakes and fruit.

The president attends the largest Memorial Day ceremony at Seoul National Cemetery. During the ceremony, a choir sings a special Memorial Day song.

On Memorial Day, the South Korean flag is flown at half-mast. Schools and businesses are closed. People visit memorials or the graves of their relatives. At 10 a.m., a siren rings and there is a minute of silent prayer all over the country. Even cars on the main roads stop for one minute.

A wall at Tagpol Park in Seoul has the names of thousands of soldiers who died.

Korean Thanksgiving

Korean Thanksgiving is a three-day harvest festival that falls in September or early October. It is a time for feasting and family. In the morning on Thanksgiving Day, people visit the place where their ancestors are buried. They clean the gravesite and leave gifts of food.

Later in the day, families celebrate by gathering for a Thanksgiving feast. The meal often includes *songpyeon* cakes, which are made of rice dough and stuffed with sesame seeds, beans, or nuts.

For fun at Thanksgiving, men have wrestling matches and women play Korean seesaw (see page 31).

At night, women and girls wear traditional dresses and perform a folk dance called *Ganggangsullae*. They sing under the full moon, hold hands, and dance in a circle.

(see page 31)

Did You Know?
Songpyeon is also called moon cake. The dough starts out in the shape of a full moon. When it is folded over the filling, it looks like a half moon.

A spicy pickled cabbage known as *kimchi* is another traditional Thanksgiving food. At harvest time, women used to make enough *kimchi* to last the winter. They stored it in clay pots underground.

National Foundation Day

National Foundation Day celebrates the creation of Korea over 4,000 years ago. Legend says a god named HwanWoong came to Earth. He met a bear and a tiger who both wanted to become human. HwanWoong told them they must stay in a cave for 100 days, eating nothing but garlic and **mugwort**. The tiger got hungry and left. The bear stayed, turned into a beautiful woman, and HwanWoong married her. Their son, Dangun Wanggeom, became King. He ruled for over 1,000 years.

The bear is a part of many Korean legends.

설악산국립공원
Seoraksan National Park

People dress in costumes resembling Dangun Wanggeom to honor him on National Foundation Day.

National Foundation Day is October 3. In Korean, it is called "the day when Heaven opened" because it honors the day that HwanWoong left Heaven for Earth. On this day, government leaders give speeches. People honor Tangun at an ancient **altar** on Ganghwa Island. They walk up to the altar on the top of Mount Mani and reenact the old ways of honoring the gods. Seven students in white dresses perform fan dances. Later, there is a torch-lighting ceremony.

Christmas Day

Christianity is another major religion in South Korea. Korean Christians celebrate Christmas on December 25. It is a national holiday where all people get the day off work and school. Many believe the Christmas season is about kindness. During the month of December, people put money in donation pots organized by the **Salvation Army**. This money goes to help the poor.

Korean children attend a ceremony by the Salvation Army to help prepare donation pots.

Colorful decorations and lights can be seen throughout South Korea at Christmas.

Korean Christians call Christmas *Seongtanjeol*, which means "the day the holy person was born." On Christmas Day, they go to church and spend the day with their families. Even Koreans who do not celebrate Christmas enjoy family time. They might volunteer to help **orphans** or to deliver food to the elderly. They will end the day with a special family dinner.

Did You Know?
To South Korean children, Santa Claus is called Santa *Haraboji*. This means Grandfather Santa. Sometimes he wears red and sometimes he wears blue!

Local Festivals

A lot of Korean culture can be seen at traditional festivals held in local villages throughout the year. These festivals often include street plays and dances. Bands might compete to be the most colorful and noisy. There are usually ceremonies where a **shaman**, or priest, asks the village's spirits for wealth and good luck in the coming year.

The colorful Mask Festival happens in Andong. People come from all over South Korea to enjoy the many traditional mask dance performances.

Sliding into a pool of mud is just one way you can enjoy the Boryeong Mud Festival. Others take part in mud-wrestling or tug-of-war during this week-long festival.

The district of Jinhae is famous for its Cherry Blossom Festival. About two million people visit the festival each year.

The Hallasan Snowflake Festival happens on Jeju Island. There are snow dancing performances on Mount Halla. At this mid-winter celebration, people enjoy the cold season by going sledding and making ice sculptures. In May, people take part in the Boseong Green Tea Festival. Boseong is the largest producer of tea in the country. People can try different types of tea, and participate in tea-leaf picking and brewing.

Did You Know?
There is a Bullfighting Festival in Cheongdo. It is a reminder that farming used to be very important to the Korean way of life. At this festival, there is a bull rodeo and a beauty contest for female calves!

Festival Games

Most holidays and festivals in South Korea begin by paying respect to ancestors. Later, they might play games, have wrestling matches, or fly kites. Some activities are only done at certain festivals, while others are traditionally done only by girls or boys.

Paengi chigi, or top-spinning, is a fun activity kids enjoy playing during Korean New Year. The goal is to try and keep your top spinning the longest.

At Korean New Year, families also enjoy playing a traditional board game called *yutnori*. Players have tokens and use special sticks as dice.

Gonggi is like the game of jacks. Players pick up five pebbles, toss them, and catch them again in the right order.

In *jegichagi*, players use their feet to keep a shuttlecock, which is similar to a badminton birdie, in the air.

Girls often play a game of seesaw during many traditional holidays. One person jumps on one end to spring the other into the air. This may have begun as a way for **aristocratic** Korean ladies to see over the walls of their **compounds**.

Glossary

altar A raised place at which people worship or leave offerings

aristocratic Of a rich and powerful part of society

Buddhism A religion of eastern and central Asia that follows the teachings of Gautama Buddha

ceremonies Formal acts performed in a certain way as part of a religious event

Christians People who follow the teachings of Jesus Christ

compounds Walled or fenced areas that contain a group of buildings

independence Freedom from control or support by others

liberation The act of freeing someone or something from control by others

movement A series of organized activities working toward a goal

mugwort An herb eaten in Korea and used in folk medicine

orphan A child who's parents have both died

protested Joined with other people to make a public display of strong disapproval

peninsula A piece of land that sticks out into the water

Salvation Army An international charitable Christian organization

scholar A person who has studied for many years and learned a lot

shaman Someone who people believe can use magic to cure sickness and control the future

rural Relating to life in the country

Index

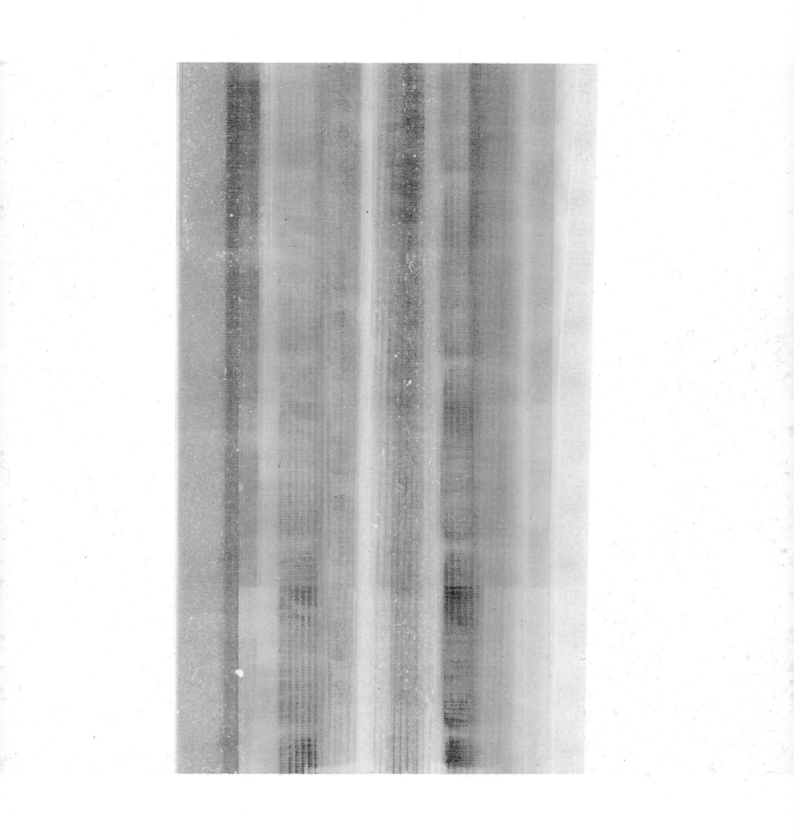